Families
and the
Secrets
They Try to Keep

Catrice Banks

ISBN 978-1-0980-6200-2 (paperback)
ISBN 978-1-0980-8620-6 (hardcover)
ISBN 978-1-0980-6201-9 (digital)

Christian Faith Publishing, Inc.
832 Park Avenue
Meadville, PA 16335
www.christianfaithpublishing.com

Printed in the United States of America

After six years of Psychology, a lifetime of dealing with different women attitudes and ten years of becoming a true woman of God, I finally made enough to have my own clinic. It was called the Bowen Center located on the corner of John and Twenty-First Avenue across the street from Fields Market. I remember when my grandmother Jeralene use to send me down to the market every Sunday to get her some sugar and cinnamon so that she could make my favorite peach cobbler. That's what she would make the family for dessert to go along with our Sunday dinner. My grandmother would reach down inside her purse, (which was big enough to fit a person's life in there) she would pull out an orange, green, and brown paper food stamp. I could just hear her now, "Make sure you come right back." Those were the good old days I thought to myself.

Although my building was not big at all, I'm truly blessed to be able to be a counselor and I believe this is my true calling from God. Today is the day of my first counseling session, and I was told I would be joined by these three women. I'm not sure what God has planned for us, but whatever it is, I trust him.

Before the ladies had arrived, I decided to get things prepared and get some paperwork done. Being this is my first actual counseling session; my stomach was beginning to feel like it was full of butterflies. So, I started praying, "Lord Jesus, oh heavenly Father, I asks that you have your way on today. During this hour and a half session, I pray for healing, deliverance, and breakthroughs. May your will be done. Amen."

Chapter 1

As I finished my prayer, I could hear the group of ladies as they entered in the building.

"Hello, is anybody even here?" one of the women yelled out. "I know this is where I'm supposed to be," she said again.

I could hear them talking loudly as I came from the back where I was finishing up praying.

"I'm here. I'm here," I repeated loud enough so that they could hear me over their own voices. "Come on in and have a seat, and, ladies, let's try and be on time next session."

One of the young ladies shouted out, flipping the long piece of hair that hung in front of her face. "I had to find a babysitter."

"That's understandable, and since it is our first session, you all get a pass," I said to each of the young ladies, putting on a serious face. "My name is Latrice Banks, and I am your counselor for the next three weeks. Can I get any of you, ladies, something to drink?" I asked.

"If you got some soda, I could sure use some," one of the other young ladies yelled out. "I'm thirsty," she said, turning her nose up as if she smelled something.

I went to grab some sodas from the little refrigerator that I kept in the back where my office was at. As I returned, I jumped right into our session.

"Being that twenty minutes has already gone by out of an hour and a half session, I want to start off by welcoming everyone in the Bowen Center. As I said before, my name is Latrice Banks, but feel free to call me Mrs. B for short. Just to give you a little background about myself, I am a life and prophetic coach. I have a master's degree in Psychology. I'm married to Curtis Banks, and we are blessed to have two beautiful children. I would like to say what a blessing it is to have you three ladies here today. I'm going to give each of you a chance to introduce and tell a little about yourself and what brought you here to the Bowen Center. Who would like to speak first?" I asked.

As I looked in front of me, I see one of the young ladies raising her hand up high in the air. "I will," she said in a loud tone of voice.

"Okay, let's start with your name and tell everyone what brought you here today."

"My name is Ebony Rose. I'm twenty-six years old. I have three kids with three different baby' daddies, and I'm a single parent," the young lady said in a very loud tone again.

I couldn't figure out if she just wanted everyone to hear her or that was just the way she spoke.

"I'm here today, to get help. I was molested by my stepfather from the time I was seven years old until I got old enough to get up and run away. Although I tried everything I could to drink the pain away to the point my body would feel numb—" Ebony Rose stopped talking in the middle of the conversation as tears started running down her face.

I got up out my seat to hand her some kleenex while trying to comfort her at the same time.

"It just seems like every time I would sober up; I couldn't help but to think about the red stains that was on my brand-new yellow sheets. I had a barbie canopy bed that was given to me for my seventh birthday that year from my mother and stepfather Chris. That was the first time he started molesting me. The red stains I can still see from the blood that would run down my leg after he was done doing his thang to me."

"What exactly do you mean when you say doing his "thang?"" I asked her.

Ebony Rose took a deep breath as she inhaled then exhaled.

I continued to try and comfort her. "It's going to be okay, Ebony. It's better to let it all out than to keep holding everything inside," I told her.

"What I meant by doing his 'thang'?" She tried carrying on. "This sick man put his penis inside of me."

It seemed like the more Ebony Rose told me, the more she cried.

Her voice became loud. "I begged him to stop." She cried even louder, "Please stop. That hurt really bad." She expressed to us. "You want to know what that bastard told me?" Ebony Rose continued, "He said, 'Everything's going to be okay. I promise,' kissing me on the forehead as he finished. I could just feel the blood running down my legs. As he began pulling his pants up, I could hear my mother calling his name. My stepfather stuck his head out the door. 'Yes, baby?' he said to my mother. She asked my stepfather Chris what he was doing in my room. Lying out the front of his mouth, he told my mother that he was on his way to the bathroom when he heard me crying, telling her that I had a nosebleed, and he was helping me clean it up, believing him she didn't even bother to come in the room to make sure that I was okay."

Ebony Rose began wiping her face as I reached over to give her some more Kleenex.

"Thank you, Mrs. B," Ebony said, trying to keep the snot from coming out her nose. "My mother just believed what my stepfather said and went back in her room. She didn't even bother to check on me, Mrs. B. The next day, I had to get ready for school. I remember my mother calling my name, rushing me to catch the bus. I could barely walk," Ebony Rose explained. "My legs were so sore. Not one time did my mother ever ask about my so-called nosebleed. How dumb could she be?" Ebony began to question. "I was only seven years old...seven years old," she repeated.

I could just hear her voice sounding weak the second time she told us.

Chapter 2

"Every night, after that dumb—"

Interrupting Ebony Rose as I could only imagine the next words that were going to come out her mouth. "I understand you're angry, but out of respect for those around us, we're not going to use profanity," I tried explaining. "I can promise you that your stepfather Chris is not going to step a foot up in here."

As we looked at each other, we all burst out in laughter. It seemed as if Ebony Rose looked in the mirror at the face expressions she was making.

"My stepfather would come in my room every night, pretending as if he was reading me a bedtime story. He was supposed to be tucking me in bed like a parent was supposed to do, but instead, he was on top of me."

It seemed as if Ebony Rose could not stop crying, so I gave her time to try to calm down. I gave the other young ladies a chance to introduce themselves.

I decided to pick who went next. So, I pointed to the young lady that had the bright red shirt with the bright red lipstick to match. "It's your turn to tell everyone your name and what brought you here to the Bowen Center."

"My name is Jessica Martin, but everyone can call me Jess. Ever since I could remember, my mother had a serious drug and alcohol problem. When she was sober, it seems like she was the best mother a person could ever want, which wasn't often."

Jessica started shaking her head as if she really didn't want to talk about it.

"Every night, mother would leave my little brother Jordan and I home by ourselves while she went out and got blasted, knowing that my brother was mentally disabled and in need of his medication, leaving me to take care of him. Jordan was six at the time, and I was only ten. I wasn't even old enough to take care of myself, let alone take care of him, but you couldn't tell my mother that. She would leave and wouldn't return until five o'clock in the morning, yelling from the top of her lungs, as she returned calling our names, Mrs. B. It's like I could almost hear her calling my name now, just yelling, 'Jess, Jordan, bring your mother something to drink.' She would just be stumbling around that small apartment that we stayed in as if we didn't have to get up for school in the next few hours."

Chapter 3

"I could just tell that she was more than drunk. Her eyes were blood-shot red."

I looked down at Jess's hands as they were shaking bad as if she had a nerve problem.

Jess carried on with her story. "My mother walks in the room that Jordan and I shared and starts beating on us with a wooden board that looks like she took off her dresser. I just remember trying to lay over my brother so that she wouldn't hurt him. She started pulling my hair, calling me every name but the child of God."

As Jessica tried to hold back her tears, I could just feel her pain, almost as if it was me.

"It's like I couldn't stop her," Jessica said, "no matter how much I cried out and begged her to stop," wiping the snot with the back of her hand before I could hand her a kleenex. "It's like I didn't even know who she was. What happened to a mother's love?" she asked. "That morning she sent us to school with bruises all over our bodies. When I got to school, my teacher, Mrs. Evans, began questioning me about the marks she saw on my face and arms. Even though I tried to lie about it, my teacher didn't have any reason to believe anything I was telling her. Mrs. Evans said she had to report the situation to the school principal, Mr. Johnson. Mr. Johnson decided to call the police and child social services. I saw the principal with Jordan in his hand. The officer was asking us to come with him. I just knew my life wasn't going to be the same. My mother was arrested for child abuse. Since we had no other siblings who would take us in to their home, Jordan and I was placed in foster care. If you ask me, Mrs. B, I wouldn't know which was worse: getting abused by your own mother or going to live with a stranger. Child social services placed us with a lady named Theresa. She seemed to be a nice lady in the beginning. It wasn't even six months that Jordan and I had been living with her. Theresa started treating us different."

Chapter 4

"One day, I asked Mrs. Theresa to help me with my homework. You know what she told me? She said, 'You're fast behind, is grown enough to be running behind those little boys out there playing around but too Dumb to do your homework.' Then she told me, 'The only reason I decided to take you and Jordan in is because I knew your brother had a mental problem, and that was just another check in my pocket.'"

When I say it took everything inside me not to go upside her head, Jessica said, "I told Theresa, 'His name is Jordan, and he has a learning disability. I told her it wouldn't be too long until we would be out of her sight."

"Okay, ladies, that is all that we have for today. Our time is up for this session. I will see each of you, ladies, next Thursday in which we will pick up where we left off. For the meantime, I will keep each of you, beautiful ladies, in my prayer. Jessica, Bianca, Ebony Rose, believe it or not, we all have a purpose on this earth. Despite your situations, I want each of you to go home and try asking God to show you what your purpose is. That's the first thing I want you to do, and I will be sure to follow up with you all. I expect to have an answer too."

That night, I went home and started thinking about the different situations that people sometimes face in life. I started praying. That's when God began to speak to me, reminding me how He can make a way out of no way.

As I sat in my comfortable recliner chair and a house full of silence, I started, reminiscing over the time, I was going through anxiety and depression. I could just remember lying down in the bed filled with fear, afraid to fall asleep, not knowing what tomorrow was going to bring me, or if there was even going to be a tomorrow. God would speak to me, telling me, "No matter what the situation may look like, just keep on going. For everything you're going through it is going to be a part of your testimony."

Chapter 5

The following Thursday, I met with the ladies for our week-two session as scheduled.

"Good evening, ladies. I'm glad to see that everyone showed up on time so that we have enough time for our discussions. We are going to just go right into this session. We're going to allow Jess to finish where she had left off, and, ladies, please tell me that you have all that were asked for you to do," I told them. "It is a part of your healing process and one of your steps to overcoming your situations. May God have his way in this place today. Amen," I said to the ladies in an open prayer.

"Okay now, Mrs. B, we're not in church," Ebony Rose blurted out.

"Ms. Ebony, church is not the only place that God could have his way. You better ask somebody," I replied. "Jessica, you may continue, and you have all ears."

Taking a deep breath, Jess decided to carry on. "After finding out that my mother was home from prison, I started sneaking over there after school. I would tell my foster parent, Theresa, that I had to stay after school to get help on my homework. I was going to visit my mother almost every day. I felt like I was finally gaining that bond like I've always wanted with her. I'm telling you she was as clean as a whistle even the house was clean. She would sit there telling me stories how my grandmother had a drinking problem, to the point, that she would forget my mother at school, and her teacher, Mrs. Tanner, would have to take her home."

Jessica began to wipe her tears away as I can see how hard she was trying to hold them back.

"My grandmother passed away from alcoholic liver disease. My mother felt like she couldn't bear, losing the only person that she had by her side, so she started drinking heavy. That's when she met, Mark, who was supposed to be her boyfriend. All along, he was the one supplying my mother the drugs. Mrs. B, my mother made a promise to Jordan and me that she would never see that man again, only for me to go over her house and out came this jerk of a man, her so called boyfriend Mark. When I walked in, my mother was laid out with white crap all on the living room table. It was like her eyes was bucked outside her head. My mother just kept calling my name, 'Jess, Jess.' I just grabbed my bags and ran out of there. I went home and just started hugging Jordan so tight. I just couldn't believe that she lied to me. I really can't believe that I allowed her to hurt me again, Mrs. B!"

I tried to comfort Jess and let her know that none of that was her fault, but looking in her eyes, I could just see that the damage was already done.

"How did that make you feel, Jess?"

"Mrs. B, I didn't visit her for weeks. After I had time to think and realized that my mother was the way she was because there wasn't anyone there for her. I was determined to help her no matter what it took."

Chapter 6

"When I got out of school that Friday, I decided to go check up on her, but when I got there, the front door was open."

Suddenly Jessica stopped talking and started screaming, "My mother was on the floor dead! She was dead! She was dead!" Jessica repeated herself over again. "My mother had white foam coming out of her mouth, and her eyes was rolling to the back of her head. When the police got there, they said she was gone, and there was nothing they could have done." Jessica cried out. "The only mother I had was gone. All I could think about was who is going to be there for Jordan and me. Ladies, all I've ever wanted was to have a mother-daughter bond with her. I just don't understand. She saw the way my grandmother was. Why wouldn't she want to be there for Jordan and me?" Falling on the floor, Jessica began breaking down. It was almost like I couldn't even get her off the floor.

In my mind, I was thinking, *Lord, what have I got myself into?* But I know I needed to be strong for these ladies.

So, I spoke up, "Although Bianca hasn't had the chance to speak yet I feel led to do this. I just want the three of you to know how brave it is for each of you to come to the Bowen Center and share your life stories. I'm going to give Bianca a chance to share with us her reason for seeking help from the Bowen Center. Before I give Bianca a chance to speak, I want each of you to know that I'm going to do everything in my power to help each one of you, to overcome the trials that you're facing today. I will also share with each of you what I did to overcome the trials that I had to face. So far, through each story that I've heard, some may be worse than others, but I can promise you, a trial is not made to last forever." See, what I can say in life, is that we all have choices.

As I'm talking, I can see the ladies, looking at me with their faces turned up, as if they knew what I was going to say was just going to make them angrier.

"Let me finish before anyone decide to interrupt me," I said to the group of ladies. "Each of you will have your turn to comment," I spoke loudly so that they would hear me clear enough. "In life, we all have choices," I repeated for the second time. "The same way you all have chosen to show up today. You also have a choice to either stay in the situation that you're in, and continue to feel how you have been feeling, allowing the trial you're facing to tear you down, or you can choose to take a stand and let your trial be your testimony and use it to help build you up so that you can start your healing process and when the time comes you could begin to help others do the same."

I could hear my voice echoing. I couldn't help but to notice that I finally had each of the young ladies' attention, trying to hold back the excitement of just thinking that it is still hope in each of these beautiful ladies' pain, knowing that I get to be a part of the change that is going to take place in their lives.

"How many of you suffered from depression because of your situation?" With no surprise, everyone's hands went up, including mine.

"You went through depression, Mrs. B?" asked Ebony Rose. "Seems like a strong woman to me," she blurted out thereafter.

"It hasn't always been that way. Trust me," I said.

Chapter 7

I could remember when I went through depression, and people would tell me the only way to get through what you're going through is by trusting in God, especially my aunt Cherry. We would be riding home from church, and she would say, "Latrice," calling me by my real name.

You must learn to believe in God yourself and know that he is able. We can't believe in him for you.

I remember looking at her, *you mean you can't just pray about it, and everything I'm going through would just go away.*

When I said that, she looked at me and said, "What good is praying for you going to do if you don't even believe that God could do it?"

I began to question my aunt because I didn't fully understand, "You mean you can't just pray for me so that my life could just start changing?" We all burst out in laughter, everyone except Bianca.

Out of nowhere, she just started yelling, "You think you got it all figured out, Mrs. B, talking all Godly? How dare you say we got a choice when I didn't choose to be raped? I didn't ask my brother to get on top of me. Where was God then when he was molesting me huh, Mrs. B?" Bianca said, crying her heart out.

There isn't no changing that. I could just see her hands and lips shaking as she carried on. There was no way I could stop her. I knew I just had to sit back and let God have his way.

Bianca continued, "My brother Mike, my oldest brother, the one I looked up to, raped me. He put his filthy fingers inside me and made me do things I didn't want to do, then turned around two years later, got into a bad car accident which killed him," wiping her face constantly. "The only two brothers that I had left blamed me for Mike's death. They didn't even want to speak to me. I was just seven years old. My mother was too busy working two jobs while my father sat on his butt with a bottle of alcohol to his mouth. Even with both parents in the house, I still felt alone. I wanted to be a daddy's girl. I did. My father cared more about drinking and my mother didn't make it any better. All she cared about was pleasing him. I am telling you, Mrs. B. all she did was work. Couldn't nobody tell my brothers that? They had it in their minds that our parents treated me better. That's why I think he started molesting me because the second nobody was looking, Mike would come into my room and shut the door talking about 'You know what time it is?'"

Chapter 8

The more Bianca would talk, the faster her hands and feet would shake. Bianca went on, "When Mike was finished, he would threaten me. He said that if I told, our father would kick him out of the house. Then he would walk out as if nothing happened. As his little sister, I didn't want to see my brother out on the streets, plus I knew if I was to tell my father, he would hurt him bad, and my father, would have told him not to never step a foot in his house again! It took everything in me not to tell my mother. In my heart, I wanted to tell somebody, but I knew she had enough stress of her own going on. I could see the bags under her eyes, and I just didn't want to worry her. So, I held it all in thinking that I could cope with it. As I got older, I began to try drinking and putting it all behind me. Somehow everything just keeps replaying in my head time and time again. What did I do to deserve this, Mrs. B? Could any of you, ladies, answer that? Huh?"

"Bianca," I called her name. "It's nothing that you did. It's not your fault. You did nothing to deserve that. Look around, Bianca. Everyone in this room has been going through something in their life no matter what the situation is. Believe it or not, you have a choice. See, ladies, I've made a choice to get up and not let my trial take over who God has called me to be, and if I had not made that choice to get back up, I wouldn't be here today. The first step to healing is being able to identify the problem. Once you're able to identify what the problem is, then you start learning how to forgive. It's important that you learn how to forgive yourself and, more importantly, forgive the person that hurt you. If you're not sure how to forgive, ladies, start praying, ask God to show you how to forgive. The only way to heal is if you forgive yourself and the person who hurt you. You want to forgive yourself for thinking that it was ever your fault for what you went through when you had no control over the situation. Then you want to forgive the person who really hurt you so that they will not have any power over you. I'm not saying that it's going to be an easy process, but what I'm telling you is it's going to be a process that is well-worth the try. The more that you forgive the person that hurts you, the less power they will have over your emotions, the easier it will become for you to move forward. For example, ladies, I started really going through depression after I was terminated from a job that I worked for ten years. I ended up injuring myself on the job. For ten years, I worked for Advance Automotive, and they waited until I injured myself and they did everything, they could to find a way to terminate me. It was to the point I got so depressed that it began to affect my everyday life.

Chapter 9

"I didn't know how to let go of what was and start living for what is. Grateful that I was able to heal from my injuries. I am blessed enough to be able to work another job. Ladies, I get where you are coming from. God had been telling me to leave that job, and because I was so worried about taking care of my family, I didn't listen. After losing my job at Advance Automotive, I sat at home angry, stressed out, and bitter, but guess what, ladies? All the stressing I was doing, allowing anger to build up in me, only caused me to lose weight, weighing my body down with stress on top of stress. Bianca, Jessica, Ebony, I began to pray and ask God to show me how to forgive that job and the people who worked there. Once I started learning how to forgive Advance Automotive, I was able to receive unemployment, which help me to get by. Not only that I started going to school for psychology, I was able to find a job that was paying twice the amount that I was making at Advance Automotive. So, listen to me when I say I get it. Healing is not an overnight process. It does take time. Think of your situation as an open wound that is trying to heal. As a wound tries to heal, it may still hurt. You may even still feel pain here and there. That doesn't mean that it is not healing. Going through this process may not feel good at first, but once you are healed, you begin to feel a lot better. The worst thing to do, is to keep reopening that wound after it has healed. What happens to a scab after you keep picking at it? (I waited for an answer, but instead, I got silence.) It eventually will get infected. Before you know it, you're going to start the healing process all over, and who wants to keep going through the same pain? So just remember, ladies, weeping may endure for a night, but joy comes in the morning" (Psalm 30:5). I will be looking forward to seeing you all next session.

Chapter 10

I would usually walk behind them, but I decided to stay back to finish my paperwork. After finishing my paperwork, I locked up the building and headed to my car. I didn't realize how long I was in that office. Must have been a little longer than I planned because when I walked in, it was light outside but when I walked out, it was dark. As I opened my car door to get in it, I could hear what sounded like two people arguing. My intentions were to get in my car and drive off, but instead, I decided to walk toward the loud noise.

As I got closer, I could see a young lady in some red high heels with a dress on that came above her knees, hanging on to a white Cadillac on rims.

"Just give me my money," the young lady said from the top of her lungs.

"I'm not giving you nothing, woman. You work for me," the man said back, yelling out the window.

"I have kids to feed, I worked for that money," she yelled.

"You're not going to do no half job with me and think you gone get paid," the man yelled back in a deep voice.

The two yelled back and forth, and before I could get close, the man in the white Cadillac with the deep voice pulled off. Then the young lady fell to the ground.

I rushed over to help her up.

"Ebony, what are you doing out here still? Our session was over hours ago."

"Don't mind me, Mrs. B, I'm okay," Ebony said.

"You're not okay. You got one shoe on and a half of a dress. Just let me give you a ride home, for goodness sake, child. It's cold out here." I placed my coat around her shoulders, and we both walked to my car in complete silence.

As I drove Ebony Rose home, I looked over and saw the hurt and disappointment in her eyes.

"Child, it's no need to be looking like that now," reminding her. "Psalm 30:5, 'Weeping may endure for a night, but joy…joy comes in the morning.' Now, Ebony, you must remember that God sees your pain. He's going to help you work through them."

Ebony Rose looked back at me and rolled her eyes.

"See you on Thursday, Mrs. B," she said as she got out of the car.

Chapter II

Thursday came around sooner than I could look up with one more session to go. I prayed that there would be healing and growth that take place in this room. May God have his way on today.

"Hello, ladies, how's everyone this evening?"

"We're doing good, Mrs. B," Ebony Rose shouted out, answering for everyone—everyone that is here, that is.

I looked around, as Ebony carried on, I noticed that Bianca was missing from her seat, trying not to interrupt her, I let her carry on, hoping that Bianca would walk through the door.

"Mrs. B," Ebony called out, "I know you're probably looking at me differently after the other night, probably wondering what I was doing. I'm going to be honest. I have mouths to feed. I have three kids to take care of, and that man owed me money."

"Owe you money? For what, Ebony? I'm not understanding."

"Just what it sounds like, Mrs. B," she said in a smart tone of voice. "If you're asking, yes, I'm a prostitute."

"Just how long have you been selling yourself, Ebony?"

"Ever since that jerk of a stepdad did what he did to me. I try to go to my mother when he was molesting me, but all she did was promise that she would take care of everything. My mother let my stepdad, rape me. I had to do something, Mrs. B. I didn't have nowhere to go. My mother didn't believe me, and I wasn't about to keep, allowing him to rape me. So, when I turned seventeen, I packed my bags, I went up in my mother's closet where she hides her money," shaking her head. Ebony Rose continued, "As I was reaching for the money, I knocked over a book, what had appeared to be my mothers diary. I opened it."

Dear diary,

it was time for me to get ready for school when my brother William called me in his room. I tried to run pass him, pretending that I was gone be late for school, but he grabbed my arm, squeezing it to the point where it started hurting, putting his nasty tongue on my neck, telling me, "You know how much your big brother love you?" In my mind, I wanted to scream out loud, but I was afraid that he was going to hit me. So, I held my tears inside. The thought of my own brother, taking interest in me, made me sick to my stomach. What kind of sick man would take interest in their own sister? I often wondered.

Ebony then turned the page and continued reading.

Dear diary,

It's the weekend, and schools were out which means my mother had to work. I knew that meant that my big brother William was going to be watching me. So, I tried to pretend I wasn't feeling good, hoping that my mother would call off, but she didn't. I tried to just go in my room and close the door, but here comes William following me. Making me lay down on the bed. It's times I just prayed that this nightmare would be over.

"My uncle William was molesting my mother, his own sister." Ebony Rose said as loud as she could. "You would think she would be the first person to believe me? I just don't understand."

"How did that make you feel." I asked Ebony Rose.

"It would help me to know that those type of men were out there. I wouldn't have felt so alone all this time, Mrs. B. I just can't believe she didn't bother to try to help me. I just couldn't figure out why my mother and my uncle Willie just couldn't get along. He was never allowed over our house." Ebony looked at me in total confusion. "The fact that she never shared with me that my uncle molested her, you would think that she would do everything in her power to make sure I didn't experience the same thing, but she didn't. She did nothing and had me thinking I was alone this entire time. I had to do something, Mrs. B. I didn't have nowhere to go. I figured if my own mother didn't care enough for me and my stepfather had no respect for me, then why would anybody else? That night, I ran away. I met this girl named Connie, who introduced me to her pimp name Mr. Charles, which was the man in the white Cadillac that you saw me arguing with. That's who I have been working for ever since. The first day I started working, I made over a thousand dollars, not every day you can go to work and put a price on it."

"Is that what you call working, Ebony?" I asked her. "What's a job when the people you're working for don't respect you or your body? You're worth so much more than that. What your stepfather did to you and the way your mother treated you were wrong. I get it, but you must learn to forgive them. I'm not telling you to forget but start working toward forgiveness and start looking forward to your future. You don't want to keep looking back, allowing your past to destroy who God has called you to be. You need to let go and let God deal with them. Ebony Rose, you have three beautiful children that need you both mentally and physically. It's time to stop hiding the pain and learn to speak out about it. Allow God to show you the way and watch how he moves. I'm not just talking, ladies. I only can speak what I know, and despite what anybody else says, it was nothing but God that help me to overcome depression, suicidal thoughts, and anxiety."

"You had suicidal thoughts, Mrs. B?" Jessica asked.

"I guess you can't judge a book by the cover."

Everyone started laughing.

"You sure can't," I replied. "I'm not going to go into all of that until next Thursday, which is our final session. I'm going to talk about suicidal thoughts and what I've experienced during the time of me going through depression. I will say during that time, I was holding a lot of things in, and I really didn't know how to let it go and allow God to handle them. I was so stressed out, to the point, I started losing my appetite and started losing major weight, to the point where it was hard for me to care for my kids and do all of the things that I were used to doing daily. Stress and depression will do a lot more to your body than you could imagine. I mean every five to ten minutes, I had to sit down from just feeling weak all the time. Believe me, ladies, I wanted to give up. I did. But who was going to take care of my kids, love them and treat them the way I would? I knew my children needed me. On top of that, if I had given up, then I would have missed out on this wonderful opportunity of being a counselor to each of you, beautiful ladies. So, trust me when I say God has a plan for your life. Everyone has a purpose here on earth. It's all about taking the time to figure out what your purpose is. It wasn't till I started seeking God that I was able to discover what my purpose was, and it wasn't till I started, believing in him that I was able to overcome it all, speaking of you, three ladies. Have either of you ladies saw Bianca? It's the end of our session, and she still has not walk through those doors."

"She usually meets me for coffee right before we come here," Jessica said. "I tried calling her, but I didn't get an answer."

"That's not like her," Ebony said. "I will stop by her house on my way home."

"Until next session, ladies. Stay blessed and less stressed."

"We will," said Ebony as she turned around and walked out the door, rolling her eyes.

Chapter 12

On the way home, I decide to go to Bianca's house to make sure she was okay. As I headed over there, I started thinking about all the brokenness that has took place in each of these ladies' lives. Then that's when my song came on "If This World Were Mine" by Luther Vandross. I couldn't help but to think, if this world was mine, I would help every broken person I come across.

Oh no, what is the police doing at Bianca's house? I hurried and placed the car in park and ran up to her house to make sure everything was all right. As I got closer, there was yellow tape placed all around Bianca's house. My heart started racing fast.

"Excuse me, sir," I said, trying to get the officers attention. "This is one of my patients' home. Do you know what happen here?" I asked.

"Not knowing what to expect. The young lady, Bianca Moore, twenty-six of age, committed suicide," the officer said, with a straight face.

"No, no, no, she would never commit suicide. You don't understand, sir. I'm her counselor. She hasn't missed a session," I said back to him in confusion.

"I'm so sorry, ma'am, but we've done everything we could," repeating himself as he walked away.

Before I could turn around, Ebony Rose and Jessica came running up to me, holding me tight.

"How could I not see the signs? Why didn't she just give me a chance? I've completely failed her. Oh Lord, why didn't I speak sooner?"

I just felt like a complete failure, at that moment, I felt like I've failed to do my job. Watching them carry her out just had me sick to my stomach.

"Mrs. B, I wanted you to know none of this was your fault. I understand why you were so hard on us," Ebony Rose said. "I want you to know that I'm going to start speaking out. The last thing we need is somebody taking their own life because of our own selfish ways."

I really want to thank each of you for trusting me to do what God has called me to do and trusting me with your stories. Your stories are worth being heard. Even when you think no one is listening, someone is listening.

Chapter 13

After the funeral, the ladies and I decided to go ahead and finish up with our last session. As Ebony Rose and Jessica headed into the room. I reminded them, "Today is our last session, and I pray that each of you receive the healing that you came for. I pray that there will be deliverance on today. May God have his way." Just so we know, I continued, "Church is not the only place that God can have his way. May his will be done on earth as it is in heaven. Amen. Good evening, ladies."

I decided to jump right into our last session. "I know it has been a rough week for all of us, being that we have lost Bianca. Today we are going to talk about suicide and suicidal thoughts. About over 830 thousand people commit suicide every year, ladies. Suicide is one of the leading causes of death. Suicide is a mental illness. It can be very common with depression. Most people who commit suicide or have suicidal thoughts are overwhelmed, going through a lot of pain and emotions. Many people commit suicide because they look at death as a way out of their situation, not realizing that when a person commit suicide, they are not only killing themselves, but they are cancelling out their future. Most people who try to commit suicide later realize how glad they did not end their life and realize that what they were experience was only getting them ready for the blessing that was about to take place, because we all have a purpose. See, Ebony, Jessica, I wasn't suicidal, but I had suicidal thoughts, which could have turned into suicide. If I had not taken authority over my life and the decisions I made. Therefore, I say that you have a choice. We all go through situations that make us want to give up, but I knew that this was not all God had for me. So, I used to pray and ask God to guide me through my situations and show me the way to get through it all. Try it, ladies, and don't be surprise when he starts talking back. In Matthew 7:7, 'Ask, and it will be given to you; seek and you will find; keep knocking, and the door will be opened to you.' I remember praying and just hearing God's voice, telling me everything that I was going through was going to be a part of my testimony one day. God told me, 'No matter what the circumstance is just pray through it all—good or bad.' He told me, 'You must learn to keep going.' I'm telling you, ladies, prayer is power, and even though you have been raped and abused, it is nothing God cannot get you through, he will never put more on you than you can bare. The 1 Corinthians 2:9 said, 'Eye has not seen, nor ear heard nor have entered into the heart of man the things which God has prepared for those he loves.'"

Chapter 14

"So you have a choice. You could either sit there singing. You shoulda, coulda, woulda, or you can stand up today and become all that God has for you to be! I would be lying if I told you it's an easy process. It's going to cost you some type of sacrifices. When I first started my walk with Christ, God told me I couldn't have sex until marriage."

"Wait, Mrs. B, you had to give up sex?"

"Oh yeah, he is tripping for real now," Ebony blurted out with one of her outbursts.

"Yes, Mrs. Rose. The Lord told me that if Curtis wanted to have sex with me, then he had to marry me. I'm being honest, Curtis and I wasn't even talking about marriage, in fact, he was one foot out the door. I'm going to tell you how God works. When God tells you to do something, you best believe he's not asking."

We all started laughing. I was glad they were listening and taking notes.

"You are telling me your man was down with that?" Jessica said with her face turned up.

"No," I said. "But I had a choice to make. I could have disobeyed what God was telling me and risk losing it all or trust in my creator who was only trying to show me my worth, something I probably wouldn't have seen in myself. The Bible does say, 'God is not a man that he should lie' (Numbers 23:19). God had been telling me that Curtis is going to be my husband. I could remember just thinking to myself like, *you sure because this man is angry*. I also knew what it felt like to be disobedient too. So, I followed the things that God was telling me to do. So, what I'm telling you two is no matter what the situation looks like, you must walk by faith and not by sight. Just because the situation is looking bad doesn't mean that's how things will turn out in the end. And I'm so glad that I chose God first because the same man who said he was never getting married was on one knee."

"I would be too if I was him," Jessica said as the two of them gave each other a high five.

"Not funny, ladies," I said. "Even after Curtis propose, we still waited. Six months later, we got married. It was one of the happiest days of my life. Ladies, what I'm saying here is trust in God, and he will make a way out of no way. I could stand here all day and tell you what God has done for me, but you must have faith and believe in him yourself. Not only that, ladies. You must want a change to happen in your life. I could remember when—"

"No, no, no, Mrs. B. Please not another story."

Both ladies stood up, waving their hands as if they were tired of hearing me talk. I couldn't do anything but laugh.

"Okay, let's be serious," I said. "It's time you, ladies, make a choice to either continue to let your situations destroy you mentally and physically, or you can allow God to show the way to whom he has called you to be."

"If it's going to get me a husband. I'll stand. I get tired of sleeping around," Ebony Rose said, trying to be funny. "Mrs. B, after seeing Bianca commit suicide, I'm making a choice to stand today. I have three kids to live for. Plus, I would never allow my stepdad to feel like he has any power over me. I know God has a much better plan for me."

As Ebony stood up, I couldn't be happier to see Jessica standing with her. I couldn't stop the tears from coming down my eyes. Although it's just the beginning for them, I could just see the changes that's going to take place in their lives.

Jessica said, "Yes, Mrs. B, I stand here in front of you, Ebony and God himself. After seeing my mother dead on the floor, I'm all that Jordan has. I refused to let my child go through what my brother and I had to go through. So, I'm making a choice today to let God have his way as you say, Mrs. B, and be all that he has called me to be.

Mrs. B, I'm having my first child. I wish my mother was here to see her first grandchild. I know she is going to be smiling down on us."

"I will say, it was a pleasure to meet each of you, ladies. Bianca, our dear friend will truly be missed. As for you two, Ebony Rose, Jessica Martin, this is our last session, but it will not be the end of our relationship that we have developed in this short period. If you ever need any help or even a prayer, I am just one phone call away. I am so proud of you, and may God be with you on your journey. Just remember, ladies, Psalm 30:5: 'Weeping may endure for a night, but joy…joy comes in the morning.'"

About the Author

Catrice Banks wrote the book *Families and the Secrets They Try to Keep* after discovering a secret in her own family. She was born and raised in Fort Wayne, Indiana. Growing up, many of us were taught that what happens in the family stays in the family. The truth is that very secret that was taught to keep is not a secret; it's your testimony.

After battling with depression and discovering that her mother went through the same thing, not only did it help her to overcome depression, but it also helped her to share her testimony. She has no longer felt alone but felt a sense of hope and a need to help others for God has prepared us for such a time like this.